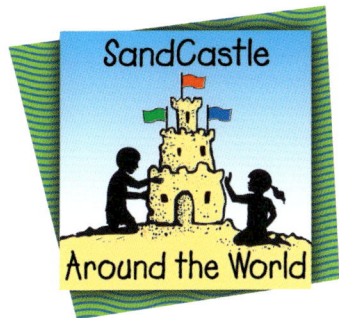

Religions
Around the World

Athens School Dist. 213
Cantrall K-3 Library
1 Braves Lane
Cantrall, IL 62625-9763

Kelly Doudna

Consulting Editor, Diane Craig, M.A./Reading Specialist

Published by ABDO Publishing Company, 4940 Viking Drive, Edina, Minnesota 55435.

Copyright © 2004 by Abdo Consulting Group, Inc. International copyrights reserved in all countries. No part of this book may be reproduced in any form without written permission from the publisher. SandCastle™ is a trademark and logo of ABDO Publishing Company.

Printed in the United States.

Credits
Edited by: Pam Price
Curriculum Coordinator: Nancy Tuminelly
Cover and Interior Design and Production: Mighty Media
Photo Credits: Comstock, Corbis Images, Creatas, Kelly Doudna, PhotoDisc

Library of Congress Cataloging-in-Publication Data

Doudna, Kelly, 1963-
    Religions around the world / Kelly Doudna.
      p. cm. -- (Around the world)
    Summary: Describes the different religions practiced around the world.
    ISBN 1-59197-568-9
    1. Religions--Juvenile literature. [1. Religions.] I. Title.

BL92.D68 2004
200'.9--dc22

2003058399

SandCastle™ books are created by a professional team of educators, reading specialists, and content developers around five essential components that include phonemic awareness, phonics, vocabulary, text comprehension, and fluency. All books are written, reviewed, and leveled for guided reading, early intervention reading, and Accelerated Reader® programs and designed for use in shared, guided, and independent reading and writing activities to support a balanced approach to literacy instruction.

Let Us Know

After reading the book, SandCastle would like you to tell us your stories about reading. What is your favorite page? Was there something hard that you needed help with? Share the ups and downs of learning to read. We want to hear from you! To get posted on the ABDO Publishing Company Web site, send us e-mail at:

sandcastle@abdopub.com

SandCastle Level: Fluent

People around the world practice different religions.

Understanding and accepting these differences is important.

It makes the world a more peaceful place to live.

Leah is Jewish.

She reads the Torah.

She lives in Israel.

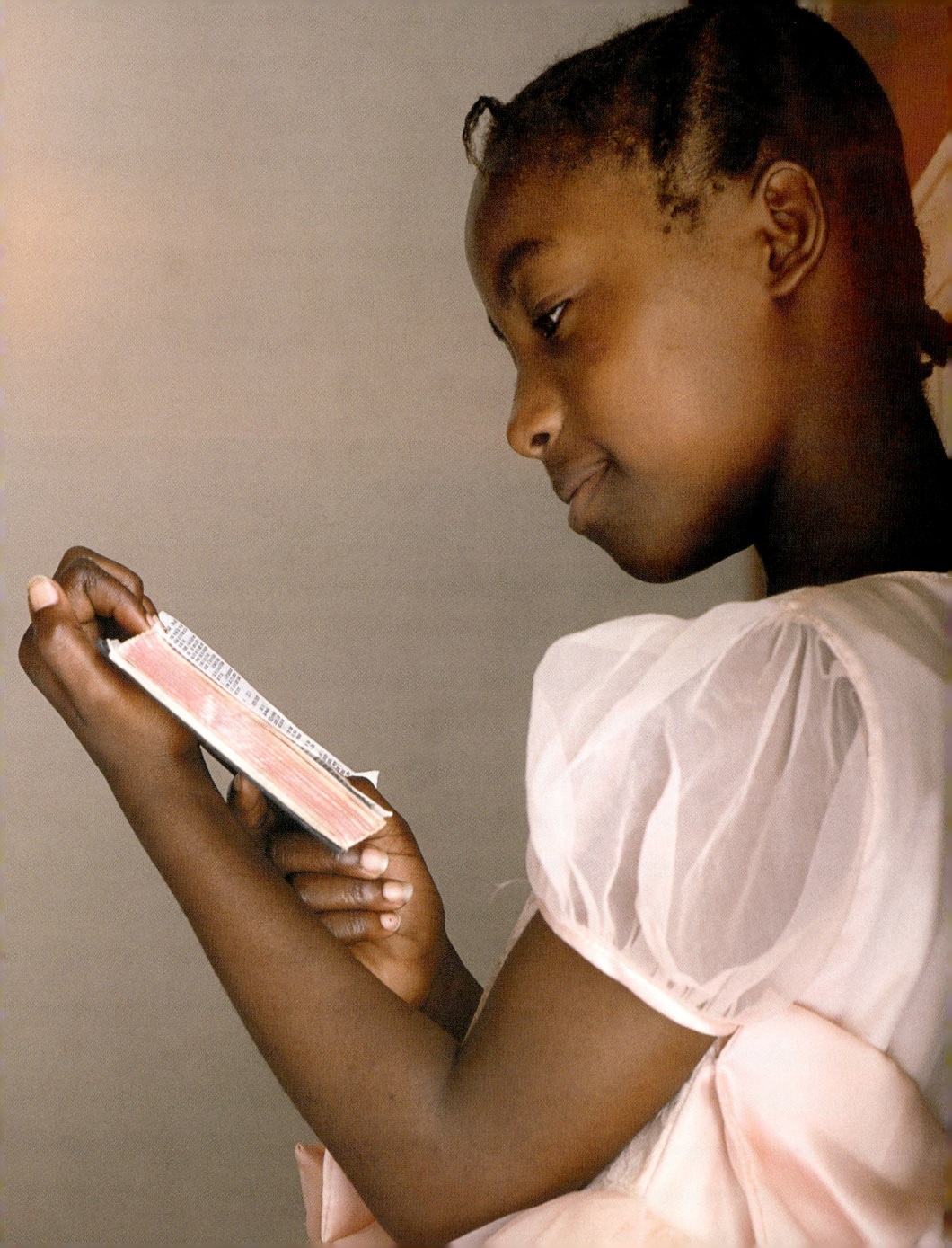

Ann is Christian.

She studies the Bible.

She lives in the United States.

Jamil is Muslim.

He learns the Koran.

He lives in Oman.

Nita is Hindu.

She reads the four Vedas.

She lives in India.

Asha is Sikh.

He studies the Adi Granth.

He lives in Pakistan.

Ang is Buddhist.

He lives by the teachings of Buddha.

He lives in Nepal.

Do you practice a religion?

Did You Know?

Yarmulke is the Yiddish name for the skullcap that religious Jewish males wear.

The Roman Catholic Church is the largest Christian organization in the world. It is found in most countries.

John and Gregory are the two most common names for popes.

Buddhist monks are not allowed by their religion to bow to world leaders.

Glossary

accept. to think of as normal, right, or unavoidable

peaceful. calm, free from disagreement

pope. the worldwide head of the Roman Catholic Church

practice. carry out or observe

religion. a set of beliefs, values, and practices based on the teachings of a spiritual leader

study. to spend time learning about and understanding something

teachings. a set of principles presented for others to accept or believe in

understand. to know well due to close contact or experience

About SandCastle™

A professional team of educators, reading specialists, and content developers created the SandCastle™ series to support young readers as they develop reading skills and strategies and increase their general knowledge. The SandCastle™ series has four levels that correspond to early literacy development in young children. The levels are provided to help teachers and parents select the appropriate books for young readers.

Emerging Readers
(no flags)

Beginning Readers
(1 flag)

Transitional Readers
(2 flags)

Fluent Readers
(3 flags)

These levels are meant only as a guide. All levels are subject to change.

To see a complete list of SandCastle™ books and other nonfiction titles from ABDO Publishing Company, visit **www.abdopub.com** or contact us at:

4940 Viking Drive, Edina, Minnesota 55435 • 1-800-800-1312 • fax: 1-952-831-1632